BLESSED KARL OF AUSTRIA:

REAL REASONS

FOR HIS SAINTHOOD

Blessed Karl of Austria:

Real Reasons

For His Sainthood

by

Zita Ballinger Fletcher

(Zita Steele)

Fletcher & Co. Publishers

www.fletcherpublishers.com

Blessed Karl of Austria: Real Reasons for his Sainthood
Zita Ballinger Fletcher (Zita Steele)

12 Star Press, an imprint of Fletcher & Co. Publishers
© December 2019, Fletcher & Co. Publishers LLC

Author: Zita Ballinger Fletcher (Zita Steele)

Interior design & type: Noël-Marie Fletcher
Cover design: Zita Steele, public domain photo
Photos include public domain images and pictures
taken by Zita Ballinger Fletcher.

Cataloging-in-Publication data for this book is
available from the Library of Congress.

Library of Congress Control Number: 2019957913

Cataloging information
ISBN-13 978-1-941184-32-5

First Edition
Published in the United States of America

Contents

Acknowledgements

Iwould like to thank the following people and places for enriching my knowledge of Blessed Karl of Austria and his wife Zita.

- Brother Nathan Cochran, O.S.B. + 2014

- Fr. Christopher Zugger

- Muri Abbey, Aargau, Switzerland

- The Museum of Military History in Vienna, Austria

- The Capuchin Church and Imperial Crypt, Vienna, Austria

- The Imperial Treasury, Vienna, Austria

- The Imperial Castle of Nuremberg, Germany

1. Purpose of this Work

Karl and Zita.

This is not a biography. My purpose in writing this book is to make a case supporting the Catholic canonization of Blessed Karl of Austria and dispel misconceptions surrounding it.

This is an expression of my opinions and beliefs as a Catholic, an author, a journalist, someone who has held Blessed Karl in great admiration for long period of my life, and as someone named after both Karl and his wife, Zita. Karl and Zita are important to my identity as a person and as a Christian. They are my role models.

There are many people in the world—Catholic and non-Catholic—that misunderstand:

- Who Blessed Karl was,

- What values he represents, and

- Reasons why there is a cause in the Catholic Church to canonize him.

Karl has been lambasted in secular media outlets, which have criticized him for being Catholic, for being an emperor, and for participating in the First World War. Aspects of Karl's life are being taken out of context.

Unfortunately, also, perceptions about Karl are becoming distorted among his supporters—many people who belong to ideological fringe groups are endorsing Karl's canonization for the wrong reasons—to the overall detriment of the cause recognizing his sanctity.

I seek to promote Blessed Karl's sainthood from my standpoint as someone against monarchy, right-wing nationalism, fundamentalism and militant Catholicism. Blessed Karl is neither a radical icon nor a political puppet.

Karl is an outstanding witness of faith and

13

valor. His heroic virtues transcend political, personal, and religious differences that divide our society today. Everyone can benefit from seeking Blessed Karl's intercession and contemplating his admirable life.

The following writings include my opinions about Karl and issues surrounding the cause for his sainthood. Also included are selected passages from blog posts I wrote as a volunteer on behalf of the Blessed Karl League of Prayers for Peace Among Nations (also called the Gebetsliga).

I hope my writings here will demonstrate that Karl was a heroic man who deserves to be recognized as a saint by the Catholic Church for his life of love and self-sacrifice.

2. Why Canonize Anybody?

Karl as a child.

To canonize a person as a saint is not to elevate them to godhood. To canonize someone is to recognize their outstanding moral character and appoint them to the status of a role model for people. In fact, to officially make someone a saint means that we recognize the person as so virtuous that we may call upon their spirit to intercede for us in our prayers to God.

Many in the world believe sainthood and "titles" as such to be superfluous. I well understand and appreciate that point of view. There have been numerous good, holy people in our world and throughout human history. Many of them were not Catholic, nor Christian, nor public figures, nor will ever be known on a grand scale or recognized by the Catholic Church or the world as "saints." I hold high admiration for many people across cultures and belief systems who stand absolutely no chance of being canonized by the Catholic Church.

However, this does not mean that Catholic canonizations have no value. It is a good thing to recognize people who have led exemplary lives, to reflect on their lives, and to promote healthy role models for others in our society today.

I have encountered people with diverse theories about who ought to be entitled to "official" sainthood—many of them display a healthy dose of skepticism about the rigorous Vatican process for canonizing a person, which seems excessive to many and ridiculous to some.

It is not my purpose here to discuss my beliefs about the broad spectrum of canonizations, how they should be conducted, or who deserves them.

There is only one canonization cause that I set out to discuss here, and that is on behalf of Karl, now a Blessed, whom I have the utmost admiration for and whose recognized sainthood I fully support.

3. A Brief Introduction to Karl

Karl and Zita on their wedding day.

Since this work is non-biographical, I suggest readers who have never previously heard of Blessed Karl to become at least marginally acquainted with the facts surrounding his life and cause for sainthood before continuing further. For the general benefit of readers, I set out the following facts about Blessed Karl from the prayer book *"Catholic Prayers to Saintly Germanic Kings & Queens,"* by Marie Noel.

Blessed Karl of Austria, Emperor & Apostolic King of Hungary

(1887-1922)
Feast Day: October 21

- Also called Charles I of Austria

- Son of Archduke Otto of Austria & Princess Maria Josepha of Saxony.

- Married Zita of Bourbon-Parma in 1911. They had 8 children. He is noted for having told her on his deathbed, "I love you forever."

- Proclaimed Emperor of Austria & King of Hungary in 1916 after the death of his great uncle Franz Joseph.

- A peace-loving and devout Catholic, he tried to bring about peace during World War I.

- Two years later, the Austro-Hungarian Empire fell; he was forced to resign but refused to abdicate since he considered his duty a mandate from God.

- He was forced into exile on a remote Portuguese isle close to Morocco to live in poverty with his family, where he died of complications from the flu.

From the Vatican for the 2004 Beatification of Charles of Austria

"Charles envisaged this office also as a way to follow Christ: in the love and care of the peoples entrusted to him, and in dedicating his life to them. He placed the most sacred duty of a king - a commitment to peace - at the center of his preoccupations during the course of the terrible war. He was the only one among political leaders to support Benedict XV's peace efforts. As far as domestic politics are concerned, despite the extremely difficult times he initiated wide and exemplary social legislation, inspired by social Christian teaching. Thanks to his conduct, the transition to a new order at the end of the conflict was made possible without a civil war. He was however banished from his country."

Pope John Paul II, October 2004:

"The decisive task of Christians consists in seeking, recognizing and following God's will in all things. The Christian statesman, Charles of Austria, confronted this challenge every day. To his eyes, war appeared as "something appalling." Amid the tumult of the First World

War, he strove to promote the peace initiative of my Predecessor, Benedict XV. From the beginning, the Emperor Charles conceived of his office as a holy service to his people. His chief concern was to follow the Christian vocation to holiness also in his political actions. For this reason, his thoughts turned to social assistance. May he be an example for all of us, especially for those who have political responsibilities in Europe today!"

[Source: *"Catholic Prayers to Saintly Germanic Kings & Queens,"* Marie Noel, 2012.]

Karl earned the admiration of many different groups of people during his lifetime. He was a humble man devoted to God and to his family. Circumstances compelled him to shoulder a burdensome responsibility he did not expect—he became an emperor, although he was far from the direct line to the throne. He rose to this challenge with a spirit of self-sacrifice and simple humility that touched the hearts of many. He remained, as ever, a loving husband and father despite the many difficult demands of his office.

He put others first. He fought for peace at a time when war was politically in vogue. He accepted international unpopularity for

21

the sake of a higher good. Mercy and bravery were evident in his actions, writings, and addresses to his people. He lived according to his conscience and died in poverty, while still doing his utmost to care for his wife and children.

4. Misrepresentations of Karl: A Growing Problem

During the course of my activities promoting Karl's canonization cause, I have come across a motley assortment of "Karl fans" who support his sainthood for some very strange reasons. Some nationalists wish to sanctify Karl the Austrian because they want to venerate a Germanic Kaiser. Karl has become a poster child for some monarchists who seemingly wish to sanctify him to promote their beliefs in government by royal dominion.

Karl—known as a humble and unpretentious man during his lifetime—also has become an icon for militant Christians who like to dress up in robes, disseminate hate speech on social media, and make fanatical displays of veneration for kingly authority. Some people among these groups self-identify as fascists.

This is alarming. It is also blindly hypocritical—Karl and his wife Zita were openhearted people who firmly worked AGAINST nationalists and fascists in their realm. In fact, Karl and Zita suffered at the hands of such people who tore their multicultural kingdom apart. Regardless of the particulars, the cause for Karl's canonization has taken on some eccentric hues due to some supporters who wish to mold Karl in their own image. Certainly, that is not what Karl's sainthood is truly about.

Some of Karl's supporters are so focused on him from a political standpoint that his canonization cause is in danger of losing its focus. This is a disservice to the memory and legacy of Karl. It grieves me deeply that Karl—falsely characterized by media during his lifetime for political reasons—should also be politically manipulated after his death.

For my part, I do not promote Karl's

sainthood because he was a king. My admiration is not for Karl the royal. Nor Karl the Austrian. Neither nationality nor royal blood are guarantors for virtue or admirable character. In my view, support for Karl's canonization should not be based upon those things.

Instead, I believe in supporting Karl's sainthood to recognize him as a heroic man. As a husband. As a father. As a hardworking professional soldier. As a patriot—not in any bigoted or nationalistic way. As a man who loved his country and worked humbly in its service. I admire Karl as a good and humble leader.

I have asked myself the painful question of whether it would be better not to canonize Karl because of the misplaced attention he receives from fanatical fringe groups, nationalists and radical right-wingers. I have grappled with the dilemma: Is it worth canonizing Karl at the risk of allowing him to become an icon for militants?

The answer I came to is that Karl must be canonized. Lots of public figures and saints have fans who support them for the wrong reasons. People can take anything and anyone out of context; this happens all the time.

In my view, it would be an injustice to Karl's legacy of virtue, hard work, and sacrifice to deprive the world of his official identification as a saint. It would prevent not only Catholics, but other Christians and people of all faiths across the world from recognizing his heroism and having the opportunity to follow his good example.

Blessed Karl is someone that would continue to have a positive influence in society if devotions to him as a saint were encouraged. What do I mean by "devotions" to a saint? It may sound peculiar, but it does not mean anything arcane or ominous. A devotion, as I mean it in this case, is a spiritual connection with a particular saint as a role model or an aspect of religious belief that plays an important part in a person's spiritual life. I myself have had a long devotion to Blessed Karl. That means Karl is a very special role model to me, and I ask his spirit to pray for me and my intentions before God.

Saints recognized by the Catholic Church often inspire people who are not Catholic and thus spread good influences in the world even beyond the reach of Catholicism. So many people are inspired by the lives and legacies of "official" saints like Mother Teresa (St. Teresa of Calcutta), St. Francis of Assisi, St. Pope John Paul II, and St. Padre Pio. Why not give the world an opportunity to be inspired by the legacy of Karl, an Emperor of Peace?

5. Karl and Pope Francis

Imust draw attention to the fact that devotions to Karl and the cause for his canonization are at risk of being derailed by growing factions within the Catholic Church.

Since the election of Pope Francis, there has emerged a distinct split between Catholics who support the Pope and those against him. Many of those who oppose the Pope do so openly and many of them are among the clergy. This appalls me, since the most basic foundation of the Catholic faith is allegiance to the authority of the Pope. The Pope is what holds the Church together. Following his example and listening humbly to his insights are what keeps the Catholic Church from splitting to pieces.

There have always been factions of Catholics who have disagreed with various Popes. There are always "armchair Popes" and holier-than-thou, self-appointed theologians. Critics on the sidelines tend to think they know better in every situation. Pope John Paul II, for example, was just "too modern" for some Catholics during his lifetime—even as others condemned him for being "too traditional." For example, there was a tremendous outcry against Pope John Paul II from some Catholics when he opposed the death penalty, even as others praised him. Pope John Paul II was his own man; he lived according to his conscience and led the Church in the way he believed best. Many of his detractors revere him after his death, and many groups who formerly admired him no longer do so. The crowd is fickle. That is why it is important for Catholics to listen to the Pope and not allow themselves to be swayed by voices of know-it-all critics. In this way, the Catholic faith holds together and continues to exist.

Pope Francis today faces a similar situation to Pope John Paul II. However, the subversive vitriol leveled at him publicly from some Catholic clergy is something I have never before witnessed. It is reprehensible.

Some of these anti-Pope figures are actively promoting Karl's sainthood cause, even as they continue to denounce the leader of the Catholic Church.

I find this troubling. Karl is a role model for the entire Catholic Church. The fact that he is being celebrated by hardliners who openly encourage sentiments against Pope Francis could, I believe, drive believers away from Karl. Catholics can easily be put off from supporting Karl's cause when they see his sainthood being promoted by clergy who preach against Pope Francis.

Karl was a person who believed in unity among diversity. He promoted peace and brotherhood among people of many different racial groups, religions and cultures in his kingdom. Karl is a saint for everyone and all Catholics should be encouraged to pray to him. His cause does not belong exclusively to a particular faction of Catholics. No matter who chooses to honor Karl, the cause for Karl's canonization is not a cause that endorses disunion with the Pope.

6. An Anti-Monarchist's Case for Karl

Karl is crowned King of Hungary.

I am not a monarchist. In fact, I am against monarchial government. I believe that monarchy is an outdated form of government that has outlived its effectiveness and has no place in modern society. I have heard that some people continue to uphold monarchy due to their belief in the esoteric "divine right of kings." Personally, I do not believe that God bestows unlimited governing rights on a set DNA pattern replicating in a particular lineage. I believe it would be unjust to impose servitude upon people on the mere basis of bloodline—requiring people to endure abuses, blunderings, and excesses from others whose only claim to leadership is genetic "royalty."

I am not the only person who thinks so or who has ever thought so, and it is thanks to this type of thinking that we have had many great advances in civilization, including steps towards constitutional government in England initiated by Oliver Cromwell, the dawn of modern China (pioneered by the admirable Sun Yat-Sen), the liberation of Russia from tsarist rule, the formation of an independent Republic of Ireland, and the birth of the United States of America. I am not a proponent of anti-authoritarianism. I believe strongly, however, that independence from monarchy is a proven good thing.

What about Karl? Since I oppose monarchy, do I hold that it was just that Karl was ultimately deposed as king and exiled? My answer is "No".

As a believer in freedom, I believe people have the right to conduct their business their own way in their own country. There is no one-size-fits-all form of government. There is no "perfect system" that works the same way for everyone, because humanity is so diverse.

I am not a proponent of international "interference"—like sending a military force to go "liberate" a country at the first public outcry. One example of misplaced "intervention" is that of the European approach to Native

Americans. European Christian settlers in America believed that Native Americans were "pagans" and that their tribal system needed reform. They attempted to Europeanize the Native Americans—eradicating their societal norms, taking away land, and forcing them to change their speech, religion and appearance. This was a travesty and destroyed many cultures and lives.

Sometimes, however, people need liberation. A good example of this is the liberation of Europe from Nazi Germany by the Allied Powers during World War II. The oppressed peoples of Europe were fully entitled to liberation from the unjust Nazi political force, and I am glad the Allied nations rose to the occasion.

During his lifetime, Karl was maligned by people who made assumptions about him because they disliked his country and political system. Some claimed that Austria needed to be "liberated." This happened especially in America, where newspapers touted that Karl was a morally bad person because he was a king. They made up false rumors and caricatured him according to stereotypes about Austrians and German rulers. They objected to his country's traditions and form of government, and used these things as excuses to ultimately overthrow his authority. This, in my opinion, was undeserved.

Karl was not an unjust ruler. In fact, prior to taking the throne, Karl was not even supposed to be a king. Karl took the Austrian crown after an unforeseen series of deaths and deposals removed a long line of successors ahead of him. Karl neither lobbied nor campaigned for political influence. He led a very private life.

Suddenly, during the First World War, Karl was called upon to become his country's leader. Karl accepted this call to leadership at what must have been a very unwelcome and inopportune time for him. It would probably have been a relief for him to stand aside and let somebody else take the job. But Karl did not shirk his duty. He recognized that his people and his country needed him.

Karl was a king who viewed himself as a servant of his people. He did not view himself as an entitled "royal" or as someone who deserved special treatment. He did not isolate himself from his subjects. Instead, Karl was a self-sacrificing man who recognized his kingship as a form of public service to others. Truly, Blessed Karl was a remarkable example of the heroic attribute Jesus described on the

Sermon on the Mount as "poor in spirit."

Karl was a hardworking, hands-on leader. Whereas many emperors avoided contact with commoners and were out of touch with their subjects, Karl didn't shy away from mingling with ordinary people in his kingdom. He often went out among them, meeting with them and talking with them about their lives and concerns.

Karl actively practiced charity. Since his youth, he was dedicated to almsgiving and assisting the underprivileged. During World War I, Karl was determined that he and his family should equally share the burdens faced by impoverished Austrian citizens. He denied himself any extra comforts or extra provisions during the war. He gave away his personal belongings—including his clothing—to people in need. Other kings might have demanded more special treatment during this hard time. Not Karl.

Karl was uncorrupted by money. Despite his aristocratic background, he did not live an opulent or avaricious lifestyle. In his office as ruler, he worked tirelessly to improve the lives of his subjects and did not spare himself from personal hardship and sacrifice. He gave away many of his own belongings to the poor, even his own clothes from his wardrobe. He also made great personal sacrifices for his wife and children, selling his ancestral heirlooms to provide for his family when they fell upon hard times.

When forced to make a home in impoverished living conditions during his exile, he did not complain. His primary concern was to continue to be, as he always had been, a good husband and father, and to serve his nation in any way he could.

Karl was a leader who viewed himself as a public servant. He treated his subjects as his brothers and sisters, and worked tirelessly on behalf of all people in his domain, regardless of creed, religion, gender, race, or ethnicity. He served everyone with equal heroic selflessness and commitment.

On this basis, I believe that Karl was one of the best kings who ever lived.

Would his descendants have followed in his footsteps? Maybe and maybe not. Bloodline is no surety for good character.

Yet, the cause for Karl's canonization is not a cause for monarchy. It is not a cause to "re-crown" a deposed emperor—nor to legitimize any of his surviving descendants' claims to royal authority.

Europe has moved on since Karl's removal from power and since the time of his premature death. Claims to the Austrian throne vanished with the death of his son, Crown Prince Otto. Europe has evolved through wars, insurrections, and political shifts from a continent once ruled by kings to a continent of nations in which common people are recognizing—and indeed demanding—their natural right to have a voice in their government.

The Habsburg monarchy is over. The Austrian Empire as Karl knew it no longer exists. Reflecting on the past era of Habsburg family dominion amounts to nothing more than misplaced nostalgia. No attempts should be made to use Karl's canonization as a reflection on the moral character of the entire Habsburg family or to make a new case for Habsburg political reign. Those days belong to Austria's past. The monarchy in Austria is over and no attempt should be made to restore it.

7. Being a Habsburg Does Not Confer Sanctity

Habsburg family members at the wedding of Karl and Zita.

Not very many people canonized by the Catholic Church were married and had children. (In my opinion, this is yet another reason why Karl should be canonized.) Across history, the lives of many admirable married couples have gone unnoticed while more of the Church's official attention has been paid to honoring people who choose religious life— this means priests, nuns, hermit,s and others who cut off human relationships in some form or another. These types of saints can be difficult for some people (including myself) to personally relate to. While these individuals are admirable in unique ways, it's not easy to directly relate to them because of their austere or isolated lifestyles. Furthermore, their physical presence on the earth seems to stop with their deaths. There are no direct descendants of Padre Pio, Mother Theresa, St. Francis of Assisi, Pope John Paul II or many others immortalized by the Catholic Church as officially recognized saints because they never married and had no children.

This is not the case with Karl; he and his wife Zita were blessed with no less than eight children and have numerous descendants. Naturally Catholics today get very eager to see the living descendants of someone like Karl who is a "candidate" for official sainthood. It's human nature to be curious, or even excited, to see and hear from someone so closely related to a personal or spiritual role model. I completely understand the reasons for the enthusiasm.

However, this excitement is leading to some very naïve assertions about the Habsburgs from some Catholics. I've heard it said that certain Habsburg descendants are "living icons" of Blessed Karl, that the Habsburgs are a "saintly family," and that the Habsburgs, as Catholics, are "models of virtue."

I could not disagree more. It is Karl who is being considered for sainthood–not his children, grandchildren, great-grandchildren, nor his aunts, uncles, nieces, nephews, cousins, or anyone else who happens to share a blood tie with him. Virtues are not hereditary. There are many examples of that in the world; just take a look at the ruling dynasties of England or France, or even ancient Rome, and you will find plenty of examples of generational moral contrasts.

While it is interesting to hear Habsburg family members discuss Karl's life and memories of him, I caution Catholics against overenthusiasm about imagined Habsburg righteousness. It makes no sense to view the entire Habsburg family and its long imperial history through rose-colored glasses. Karl's virtues must be attributed to him as an individual.

8. The "Peace" Ruler

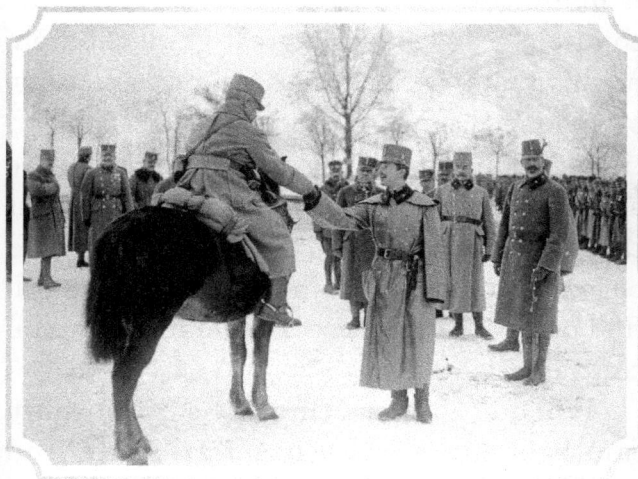

Karl, as an emperor of Austria, was known in German as a Kaiser. Perhaps the word "Kaiser" conjures images of mustachioed men with steel helmets and frightening glares—if so, such associations would be justifiable. Many Kaisers in history were known for being belligerent and martial characters. Karl, however, was completely different as a Kaiser. The difference in his behavior from previous rulers was so remarkable that his subjects widely noticed it and nicknamed him the "Friedenkaiser"—the "peace emperor."

This epithet might sound childish or superficial. It is not. To be called "a peace emperor" in a historically proud Germanic nation like Austria is a very significant phenomenon. But in order to understand that significance, one must first understand Germanic warrior culture and a few things about Kaisers in general.

As someone of German heritage, I would like to offer a few words to describe Karl's virtuous behavior in a cultural context—while at the same time avoiding stereotypes. I've heard others dismiss Germanic people with such phrases such as, "Those Germans are all warlike," or "They are all racists." That is too broad of a brush to characterize any group of people, and I believe it is inaccurate. Broadly speaking, I would describe Germanic culture as generally valuing the virtues of strength, discipline, industriousness, and intellectual independence—and, of course, the elusive and almost intangible quality of "Germanness"— which is unsurprising since it is human nature to admire aspects of the self and one's native culture. Kaisers, however, tended to magnify these "values" to the extreme.

Zita Ballinger Fletcher

*Statues of warriors and military figures
outside the Imperial Palace in Vienna.
Photo by Zita Ballinger Fletcher.*

No Kaiser in history was ever known for
being an activist for peace. Kaisers historically
styled themselves as idols of war. For a
Germanic emperor, being aggressively warlike
was perceived as a virtue. For centuries, Kaisers
ruled as conquering warriors, attributed
with deific characteristics. They cultivated
overbearing strength, coldness, aggression,
and sternness in excess. Many were racist and
intolerant. Emperors were unsparingly strict
with subordinates and known for being harsh
even to their own family members. They did
not take a hands-on approach in relating to

their subjects—instead, they customarily portrayed themselves as distant fatherly figures, always making it clear they were mighty and superior. They lived in luxury and kept away from common people. They showed neither personal empathy nor mercy towards their enemies.

However, I must point out that the phenomenon of warlike rulers is not unique to the cultures of Austria or Germany— similar situations have occurred worldwide throughout history. Notably aggressive and harsh rulers have hailed from many countries including Japan, China, Greece, Mongolia, Scotland, Ireland, Russia, the Middle East, various indigenous tribes, and other nations.

To illustrate Karl in historical context, let us examine two examples of very different Kaisers who lived during the same time period as Karl:

• Kaiser Wilhelm II of Germany, who ruled during the First World War, and

• Kaiser Franz Joseph of Austria (Karl's predecessor as emperor).

Both men cultivated lofty attitudes, cultural coldness towards non-Germanic races, and militarism.

Kaiser Franz Joseph of Austria was known

for being harshly militaristic. He made much of his military career and commissioned paintings depicting his exploits on various battlefields. These paintings can be seen today in Vienna. At home, he had stormy relationships with his family members—most notably with his hot-tempered Bavarian wife Elizabeth (nicknamed Sisi) and his nephew Franz Ferdinand. The Kaiser never forgave Franz Ferdinand for marrying a woman of lower social rank. After Franz Ferdinand and his wife were assassinated in Sarajevo, the Kaiser refused to take pity on their remains—he forbade an imperial funeral and cruelly "banished" the bodies to an estate far from Vienna.

Another coldhearted Kaiser was Wilhelm II of Germany. Kaiser Willhelm II was legendary for stomping around in boots, wearing winged and spiked helmets, and breathing bloodthirsty proclamations to the point of being ridiculed internationally and even among his own people. His beloved daughter, Victoria Louise of Prussia, styled herself as a modern Valkyrie, galloping around with her father's cavalry and proudly wearing a hat bearing the Totenkopf "death's head" skull-and-crossbones symbol. This ancient symbol of death was later adopted by the infamous Nazi S.S. troops during the

Third Reich era, who murdered civilians and created concentration camps.

Contrast these two examples with Karl, the "Peace" Kaiser. His subjects and his family members knew him to be an openhearted and loving person. He did not cultivate hatred—not among his soldiers, officials, at home, or among his children. He did not promote symbols of death. He did not encourage his family to be cruel or intolerant. Karl would never have "banished" a family member because of their marriage nor discriminated against a person due to their social status. He had every opportunity in World War I to issue aggressive edicts like Kaiser Wilhelm II—instead, Karl issued unending calls for peace.

To make an even bolder contrast between Karl and other Germanic rulers, I would like to contrast Karl's methods of rule with the "Kaiser-like" behavior affected by Adolf Hitler of Austria. Hitler and his fanatical Nazi followers literally attempted to make a religion out of being German and worshiped their own political regime. They drew inspiration from Wagnerian operas, folk tales, and legends of powerful German kings of former times. The Nazi idea of leadership was not a Christian one. It was a model of rule without hope, love or mercy. As "the Führer," Hitler essentially crafted himself into a socialistic version of a German Kaiser. He tried to establish a "Reich"—an empire—and affected imperial behavior without directly using the title of king. In keeping with previous traditions of Kaisers, Hitler presented himself as a sympathetic "fatherly" figure to his followers—a lofty, dignified character who valued calculated cruelty and was merciless to his enemies.

We all know that, to the horror of humanity, Hitler was extremely popular in Germanic countries and among his own people. So were previous Kaisers. Their distorted representations of callousness as discipline, hostility as strength and hatred as honor warped people's minds and won the fleeting favor of crowds. National pride transgressed the boundaries of human decency. These leaders incited their people to wage war— leading to atrocities that permanently scarred the world and left entire civilizations in ruins.

Contrast this attitude with the approach of Karl, the ruler of peace. Karl could have taken a similar road to the leaders previously mentioned. He had a royal pedigree and distinguished ancestors to boast of. At the time of his ascent to the throne, Karl was a dashing young man in a uniform. He was photogenic. He had a military background. He had a glamorous wife. People liked him. His coronation was met with much excitement. War was raging and the eyes of the whole world were on Karl. He could easily have exploited it. He could have fanned the flames of conflict and stirred up his subjects by ranting against political opponents, organizing rallies and marches, and inciting people to fight. His people would have followed him aggressively and willingly if he had inflamed their pride and passions to spur them to wage bitterer war.

However, Karl acted according to his strong moral convictions and Catholic faith. Karl declared that his priority was to seek peace. He made the pursuit of peace his number one policy during World War I.

Peace was an unpopular move. Some Austrian government officials liked the old way of doing things and would have liked to transform Karl into a new Franz Joseph. Internationally, Karl was ridiculed. His words and policies made him a laughingstock. There was no end to the unflattering publicity he received from his political opponents in Europe and elsewhere, who constantly poked fun of him and dismissed him. His commitment to peace also irritated his German allies, who were eager to keep fighting.

Yet Karl, despite all of this pressure, did not change his position or retract his views. He did not deviate from his plan to treat all nations with respect and achieve peace, which he viewed as his responsibility to his people.

This proclamation written in German and issued by Karl in 1918 (translated by me into English below) demonstrates that Karl identified with his subjects and was personally engaged with ordinary people. Karl chose to walk a completely different path, abandoning the traditional role of "warrior" and "god-emperor," and choosing to seek peace.

"February 12, 1918

"To my People!

"Thanks to God's gracious assistance, we have made peace with Ukraine. Our victorious weapons and our sincere peace policy, which has been pursued with unrelenting endurance, have reaped the first fruits of our defensive struggle which is being conducted for our self-preservation.

"In unity with my severely tested peoples, I trust that after this first and very gladdening peace agreement, the general peace for all of humanity will soon be achieved.

"Under the auspices of this peace with Ukraine, our gaze turns with full sympathy towards this ambitious young nation, whose hearts were the first among our enemies in which the feeling of charity became active, and which, after having demonstrated proven courage in numerous battles, also committed to sufficient self-restraint in order to express their better convictions to the world through example...

"As from the very first moment I ascended to the throne of my illustrious ancestors, I have felt united with my peoples in the self-evident resolution to fight our way out of this forced struggle until the achievement of an honorable peace, I also feel all the more united with them in this hour, in which the first step towards the realization of this goal has now taken place.

"With admiration and heartfelt recognition for the almost superhuman endurance and unparalleled spirit of self-sacrifice of my heroic troops, just as for those at home who daily make no lesser sacrifices, I look with full confidence to a near, happier future.

"May the Almighty continue to bless us with strength and endurance, so that we can achieve the final peace not only for ourselves and our loyal allies, but also for the entire humanity.

"KARL"

Please note Karl's reference to the war as a "forced struggle." That is extraordinary. A Kaiser figure like Wilhelm II, Hitler, or even Franz Joseph probably would have referred to war differently and in more glamorous terms—perhaps using words like "glorious struggle," "Sieg heil!", "total war", or "final victory", which the world heard from Germany often during World War II. That would have been the popular and traditionally acceptable way for a Kaiser to refer to a war he was fighting.

But Karl was honest. He risked being labeled as "weak" by admitting to the entire world that he did not want a war—that it was something being "forced" upon him and his people, and that all his efforts were directed not at winning it, but bringing it to a peaceful end. Karl viewed achieving world peace and the wellbeing of his people as the supreme goals of his leadership as a king and as a military commander.

During the war, Karl visited and interacted with ordinary people in his country—no matter who they were, what social status they had or what religion or ethnicity they belonged to. He did not lock himself up in a palace, hide in a bunker or demand that his staff solve all the country's problems. Instead, he personally met and interacted with people in all levels of society to address their needs. He took personal responsibility for improving the lives of people who depended on his leadership. He appeared in so many places at such short notice that people gave him the nickname: "Karl the Sudden."

Karl did not surround himself with fashionable celebrities or fans of royalty; he did not cut himself off from common people. Karl was humble and interested in improving the lives of others around him. Karl took a hands-on approach to helping people. He treated everyone with kindness.

Although he was Austria's last emperor, Karl shines out as a lone member of a powerful dynasty who dedicated himself not to rivalry or conquest, but to peace and goodwill towards all nations. He continues to go down in history not as an emperor of war, but as the Friedenkaiser—a ruler of peace.

9. An Advocate for Cultural and Religious Tolerance

Some of Karl's predecessors ruled with a bias against certain religious and racial groups in the realm. The former Austrian Empire was very multicultural—filled with many diverse people, such as members of Polish, Czech, Hungarian, Ukrainian, and other Eastern European communities. It was also religiously diverse—home to many Eastern Rite churches and a large Jewish population.

Over the centuries, the Austrian monarchy expanded its control over diverse territories and brought many of these ethnic and religious groups into submission. Austrian monarchs tended to favor the German majority culture and historically showed less respect to the many different Eastern European populations in the kingdom.

Historically, relations between ethnic Germans and Eastern Europeans were poor, as were relations between Catholics, Jews, and Eastern Rite churches. Some Austrian monarchs had very difficult relations with Hungarians due to racial prejudices and lack of communication.

This was not the case for Blessed Karl. From the moment he became king, he viewed himself as a public servant with important responsibilities to everyone regardless of their religion or background. He devoted himself to healing past relationships with Eastern Europeans in his lands—especially the Hungarians—and building on those relationships to bring about peace.

In fact, he placed such great emphasis on healing past wounds with ethnic minorities that he voluntarily participated in Eastern European customs, wore traditional Eastern European clothing, and had his children taught to speak Slavic languages from their earliest years. He personally reached out to members of the Austrian Jewish community, who were historically very mistreated, and became a strong advocate for Eastern Rite churches. He did not make moral or racial distinctions about anybody. He valued all people whom God called him to serve.

Today, Karl is fondly remembered by the many diverse people whom he served with such unparalleled dedication. Even today, his picture—be it in the form of a carving or icon—is displayed by members of Czech, Polish, Hungarian, and Ukrainian cultures, and shrines in his honor exist in Eastern Rite churches.

No other Austrian emperor has ever earned this distinction.

10. An Inspiring Commander

Karl salutes soldiers in 1917.

To be a soldier was Karl's vocation. Biographers say Karl was attracted to military life from a very young age. As a boy, he played with model soldiers and was keenly interested in the military careers of some of his older relatives. Karl voluntarily chose a career as a professional soldier.

Karl's decision to pursue a military career was noteworthy. As a royal family member, Karl was not obligated to pursue a profession. Royal family members often held titles and positions for show, but were not committed to working as dedicated professionals. Karl was a rare exception. He worked at various military posts. Spurning the luxuries enjoyed by many of his relatives, he dedicated himself to his career and enjoyed marching, drill and cavalry exercises. For much of his life, he lived in military housing—even as a married man, with his wife Zita and their many children. After becoming emperor, Karl continued to live a simple life with his family.

Karl strongly identified with his fellow soldiers. He was constantly with his frontline troops during World War I. He toured many places along the frontlines. He took time to personally speak with and decorate soldiers fighting for the Austrian Empire for the many diverse ethnic and regional backgrounds.

This was unprecedented behavior for an Austrian Kaiser—throughout Austria's history, aristocratic military leaders viewed themselves as too lofty to mingle with common soldiers. But Karl knew no classism.

Karl also took the time to write personal messages to men under his command during World War I. This, also, was rare—Germanic emperors historically usually gave harsh orders, rather than candid personal addresses to fighting troops.

In his messages, Karl addressed soldiers under his command as comrades and fellow patriots rather than subordinates. He did not incite them to fight using hostile language or provocations against the enemy. Instead, Karl spoke of his intense awareness of his men's sufferings and those of their families at home, and promised to do all in his power to work for peace.

Karl's sincere devotion to his men and fellowship with them inspired deep loyalty among them—especially among men from the Eastern regions of his territory who had never before been treated warmly by Austrian commanders-in-chief.

Some of the soldiers Karl spent time on the frontlines with included Hungarians, Austrians, Czechs, and Poles.

During one such visit, one Polish soldier in the Austrian Army was so inspired by Karl's exemplary personal leadership that he named his own son after Karl—this son was Karol Josef Wojtyła—who became Pope John Paul II. Pope John Paul II shared the story of his namesake and had great admiration for Karl, whom he praised in a 2004 beatification homily as a "Christian statesman" who "conceived of his office as a holy service to his people."

To this day, Karl's memory as a just and virtuous soldier lives on as an inspiring example of patriotism, humility and public service.

11. A Loving Husband

Karl and Zita were married on Oct. 21, 1911, after a brief courtship. They enjoyed a happy union for 10 years. Their love withstood the ravages of war, gossip, and political strife. They strongly supported each other and had the courage to raise a family amid the turmoil, having eight children together.

Karl was a strong and brave man. He enjoyed many healthy, typically masculine pursuits like hunting, horseback riding, military exercises, and driving cars. However, he was not a chauvinist. He did not affect swaggering pretenses because he was Catholic and male. He was neither conceited nor insecure about his masculinity. He did not prohibit his wife, Zita, from making public appearances, accompanying him in the duties of his office, or expressing her opinions about political matters. Karl did not keep his wife confined at home. He did not command her to trail meekly behind him. Zita was not the type of woman to hover quietly in the background—she was intelligent and spirited, and her husband loved that about her. Karl and Zita shared a relationship based not on gender-defined dominance, but on mutual admiration and love.

Zita and Karl were inseparable during their lifetime. They always traveled together and were always photographed side by side.

Zita visits a field hospital during World War I while Karl is reviewing troops nearby.

The couple shared many common interests, including their religious faith. Karl proposed to Zita at the Shrine of Mariazell in Austria. They inscribed a prayer to the Mother of God on their wedding rings, *"Sub tuum presidium confugimus, sancta Dei Genitrix".* ("We fly to take refuge under your protection, O Holy Mother of God.")

Zita's brave, selfless devotion to her husband is what I admire the most about her. She accompanied her husband everywhere and supported him in all his heavy responsibilities. She was with him on Nov. 21, 1916, when

63

he became the Emperor of Austria after the death of his great uncle Franz Joseph I. She even traveled with him to battlefields during the First World War. Zita remained courageously at his side during his times of political unpopularity and poverty. She took care of him unceasingly during his final illness and death in exile. Empress Zita's motto was: "Plus pour vous que pour moi" ("More for you than for me")—a statement she demonstrated to her husband Karl with her life; this is one of my favorite things about Zita, who is my namesake.

This motto is inscribed on a wall plaque at the burial place of Karl and Zita's hearts at the Marian chapel to Our Lady of Loreto in Muri Abbey, Switzerland. I was deeply touched and honored to be able to visit the shrine there in 2017.

The loving couple was separated at death. Zita's body is buried among the Habsburg imperial family in the Capuchin Crypt in Vienna, while Karl's body remains at the site of his exile on Madeira in Portugal. Karl's last words to Zita were: "I love you forever."

Although they are interred separately, their hearts are buried together at Muri Abbey. This is a moving testament to their eternal love.

The custom of heart burial was common in Europe, especially during the Middle Ages. The heart was often separated from the rest of the body due to the spiritual significance of the heart and also the fact that it was easy to transport to distant places. Hearts are usually stored in special vessels and interred in places of great importance to the deceased. Heart burials were also a long-standing custom of the Habsburg royal family.

Karl and Zita's hearts are buried together behind this altar in Muri Abbey. Photo by Zita Ballinger Fletcher.

Muri Abbey, dedicated to St. Martin of Tours, is a Benedictine monastery near Basel, Switzerland. It was founded in 1027 A.D., built with the support of the Habsburgs, and inhabited by Benedictine monks for over 800 years. The church interior is today one of the most impressive examples of religious baroque architecture in all of Switzerland.

The hearts of Karl and Zita are enshrined behind the altar in the Loreto Chapel—a small and simple chapel near the monastery garden—in keeping with their devotion to each other and their faith in the Holy Mother of God. Overlooking the tiny room is a picture of Our Lady of the Bowed Head, the couple's favorite religious image during their lifetime. A bust of Karl stands in the corner near a small prayer space for visitors. Plaques on the wall memorialize the life and endless love of the couple.

12. A Helpful Example for all Families and Relationships

Karl waves at Zita.

Because of their happy marriage, Blessed Karl and his wife Zita are often viewed as models of an "ideal" family.

But many of us in the world cannot describe our own families as ideal. We humans are far from perfect. Many people do not come from happy homes. Many are divorced, separated, single, or in complicated life situations. Also, it is worth noting that the outward appearance of a stable home or marriage does not equal happiness. Many people get into relationships for the wrong reasons and are unhappy. Sometimes people are suffering under a calm surface. You cannot judge families or marriages by outer appearances.

We know from all evidence that Blessed Karl enjoyed a good marriage and home life. What was the key to the happiness in his domestic life? What do people admire about it?

There is only one answer: love. And on this basis, I believe that Blessed Karl is a good role model for anyone and everyone—no matter what life situation or relationship status. We can learn from Blessed Karl's example how to truly value, accompany, and care for others in our lives.

Blessed Karl put true love into practice. Everyone can ask for his prayers in Heaven and for him to be a spiritual role model and helper in their lives.

13. A Good Father

Karl with one of his sons.

Sources tell us that Karl was a very engaged father who cared deeply for all of his children. He was active in their upbringing despite the many pressures and duties demanded by his office. Karl provided hands-on care for his children and had a role in their education.

It would have been easy for a busy professional man like Karl to shrug off all responsibilities of child-rearing by saying he was "too busy" and had no time to deal with the demands of growing children—his time certainly was very limited, but Karl always made time for his family because he loved them. Or, like other German aristocrats, Karl could have taken a sexist approach and abandoned all child-rearing responsibilities to his wife as "women's work." Karl's own father was absent for long periods during his childhood. Karl did not take this approach.

Assuredly Karl was very stressed due to the war and his pressing duties as a political leader. Did he vent his stress on his family and demand to be "left alone?" Did he whine, yell or throw fits? Did he emphasize that his time was more important than that of others, or treat his children as if they were annoying inconveniences? Did he mistreat his wife because she was constantly pregnant during times of war and poverty? Did he use his hardships as excuses to indulge himself, or blame stressful situations on his family?

No, Karl did none of these things. Karl's deep and sincere love for his wife, Zita, was reflected in his love and care for her and their children. Accounts tell us that Karl was a very kind and warmhearted person who also possessed great self-discipline and strength of character. As a father, Karl made sure that his children knew that he loved them. He went out of his way to be engaged and caring towards them despite the stresses and hardships in his life. His children and his wife were his treasures. He did not complain about them. He was not a negative person in his home life. He did his best to provide for his family without any hesitation.

14. Love: Karl's Strongest Virtue

I believe that love was Karl's strongest virtue. Indeed, love was something that Karl was devoted to in a religious sense. The image of the Sacred Heart of Jesus was a very important facet of Karl's prayer life.

This is interesting because images depicting Jesus's Sacred Heart were not common during Karl's lifetime. Nowadays we take them for granted. However, back then, images showing the Sacred Heart were very unusual. Images of and prayers to the Sacred Heart of Jesus did not become widely popular until the Catholic Church promoted the devotion for the general public starting in 1899, two years after he was born.

Karl was very attracted to the image of the heart of Jesus. The heart of Jesus represents God's love. This image held great significance for Karl. The picture of God's Heart was one that Karl and Zita always kept close by, in their home and when they traveled. The Sacred Heart image also appeared on Karl's memorial prayer cards distributed at the time of his death.

The image of the Sacred Heart of Jesus was an inspiration to Karl in his private and public life. God's love shown in the image of the Sacred Heart of Jesus was an example that Karl followed. Love is evident in Karl's actions. Karl truly lived a life of love for his wife Zita, love for his family, and love for his people and his country.

15. Karl in My Life

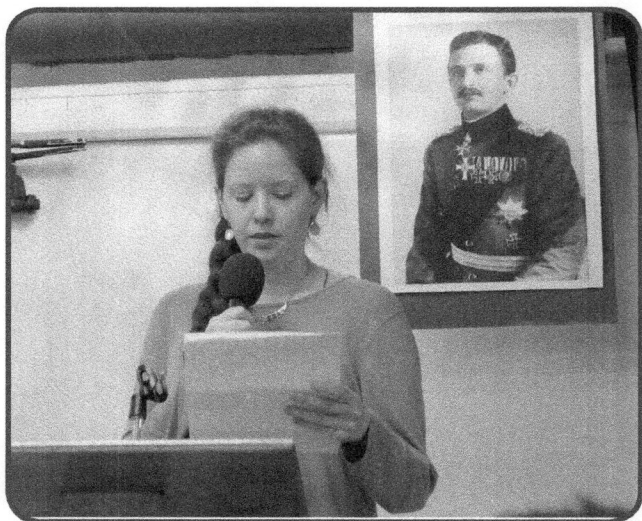

The author gives a presentation in 2018 about Blessed Karl as her role model.

Blessed Karl was present in my life before I was born. This unusual story begins in 1989, the year of Empress Zita's death. My parents were journalists working in Beijing, China. They had been married for two years. My father was a photographer for Reuters. My mother was a China correspondent for a Wall Street newspaper. One day my mother saw a headline in the International Herald Tribune newspaper from the Associated Press that caught her attention.

A copy of the 1989 newspaper article that led to the author being named after Empress Zita, taken from the author's scrap book.

"Zita, Last Empress of Austria, Dies in Swiss Exile at 96."

"ZIZIERS, Switzerland—Zita, 96, the last empress of the Hapsburg Empire, who played a role in a plan to end World War I and was subsequently exiled from Austria, died Tuesday.

"Born May 9, 1892, in Pianore Castle, near Pisa, as a princess of Bourbon-Parma, Zita was the widow of Karl I, the last crowned head of the Hapsburg dynasty, which ruled for 640 years. She died at Johannes-Stift, a home for the aged in Ziziers, a village on the Upper Rhine. A spokesman for the House of Hapsburg, Bernd Posselt, said Zita "just faded away" after ailing for some time. ...

"Karl I, who became emperor on the death in 1916 of his uncle, Franz-Joseph, initiated moves that year to negotiate a peace he hoped would save the Austrian monarchy. Zita helped arrange secret contacts with the Allies. The go-between was her brother, Prince Sixtus of Bourbon-Parma, then serving in the Belgian Army, who was in touch with President Raymond Poncare of France. In turn, Poincare notified King George V of Britain.

"The Austrian efforts were revealed in 1918, causing an uproar and rocking the Austrian-German alliance. ...

"After the victory of the Western Allies, he agreed to "temporarily relinquish" his imperial rights, but never officially abdicated.

"A long odyssey began for Karl and Zita. Initially, they went into exile in the Lake Geneva chateau at Prangins, from where Karl began two attempts to recapture the Hungarian throne. The Allies banished the family to Madeira in 1921, where Karl died of pneumonia a year later.

"A widow at 29, Zita turned down invitations from royal relatives and instead chose to bring up her children in modest environments, first in a Spanish fishing village and then in the Belgian countryside.

"When Hitler moved to annex Austria, her oldest son, Otto, the new head of the House of Hapsburg, urged the Western allies to intervene, which cause the Nazis to issue an order for his arrest. The family fled to Canada and then to the United States…

"After World War II, Zita toured American cities to promote humanitarian aid for Europe. In the early 1950s, she returned to Europe and settled at Ziziers…"

My mother had never seen the name Zita before, and it caught her attention. She was so impressed with the beauty of Zita's name and the heroism of her life story that she decided instantly after reading this newspaper article that, if she ever had a daughter, she would name her Zita. I arrived unexpectedly one year later.

Thankfully, I was named Zita despite strong objections from some people on my father's side of the family, who disliked my name because they thought it sounded "too foreign."

Zita is, in fact, an unusual name here in the United States. Many people I meet here have never met anyone named Zita before. Some presume that Zita is a nickname. Others, mostly Catholics, recognize the name as that of St. Zita of Lucca, Italy, the patron saint of cooks. Many have incorrectly assumed that St. Zita of Lucca was the person I was named after.

I grew up very aware of the fact that I was named after Empress Zita and the reasons why I was named after her. I have always been very happy with my name and proud to be named after such a courageous woman. However, I did not know the details of Empress Zita's life story until later, when I was a youth in high school.

When I was about 14 years old, I received a biography of Blessed Karl and Empress Zita called, "A Heart for Europe," by James and Joanna Bogle as a Christmas present. I was making a transition from middle school to high school during that time and had other things on my mind, such as enjoying school breaks and amusing myself with sports and hobbies before having to study again. I was not in the frame of mind to read history books. I ignored the book for several months. Then one day, I started to read it.

I was not able to put the book down. I was so impressed with Blessed Karl. It was the first time I had read anything about him. He was a man with all the virtues I greatly admire— particularly his self-sacrificing love for his country, his family and his wife Zita.

I was not old enough to receive the Sacrament of Confirmation, which would make me an official adult believer in the Catholic faith. For Confirmation, Catholics receive a special anointing recognizing they are full members of the Church. Catholics who decide to get "confirmed" are supposed to reflect on their religious beliefs and choose a saint to "name themselves" after. This saint is supposed to serve as a special role model in the person's spiritual life. I knew, even before I finished reading the book, that I wanted Blessed Karl to be my chosen namesake and saint role model as a Catholic believer.

Several maternal family members strongly objected to my decision. They had never heard of Karl before. When they found out more about him, they disliked the fact that he was Austrian, a statesman, and a soldier. They also objected to the fact that I was choosing a male role model. They wanted me to choose a girl saint instead. They suggested a variety of "nice" female saints—with whom I had nothing in common and cared nothing about. As a last-ditch attempt, they tried to persuade me to choose St. Michael the Archangel—a longtime favorite saint of mine. Their efforts were in vain. Karl was special to me—Karl is someone with all the virtues I admire the most. I was determined to take his name in Confirmation and my choice was immovable.

My Confirmation Namesake

BLESSED

1887   1922

Karl Habsburg

by Zita Fletcher, Confirmation Year III

Cover page of the author's Confirmation saint biography, which she created and submitted prior to receiving the Sacrament.

The following is an excerpt from a document describing my Confirmation namesake, which I presented to local Catholic authorities for approval before I got confirmed:

FROM MY CONFIRMATION Document, *(written in 2006):*

"The saint I have chosen to be my Confirmation namesake is Blessed Karl von Habsburg of Austria, the last ruler of the Austro-Hungarian Empire. ...

"I knew from the moment I finished reading his biography that I wanted Blessed Karl to be my Confirmation namesake. Though he was an Emperor and the member of a great and wealthy royal house, he remained pious and holy and did not allow himself to be governed by riches. He kept his faith and his courage even in the face of slander, ostracism, exile, and death. He sacrificed his life and put aside all personal wants for the good of his family and of his country. I consider him a hero and my role model and have a great devotion to him. He is a wonderful example of bravery and dedication, and his life is a lesson to us of how all Catholics should always include God in their lives."

I was not sure if I would be allowed to choose Karl's name, since he was not an official "saint" and had only recently been made a "Blessed." Oh well, I thought—if they won't let me choose

Karl because he's "only a Blessed," I just won't get confirmed! There was no compromise in my mind. Thankfully, my choice was approved and I was confirmed on April 23, 2006–on St. George's Feast Day–with the new Catholic name "Zita Karlotta," resulting in me being named after both Karl and his wife.

Zita *Karlotta* Ballenger
Fletcher

received the

Sacrament

of

Confirmation

on
Sunday, April 23, 2006

---

*Copy of the author's Confirmation
certificate showing she is named after
both Karl and Zita.*

During my life's journeys, which have taken me to many different places, I have always sought to remember Karl and Zita wherever I could. When I was in Europe, I visited Empress Zita's final resting place in the Imperial Crypt in Vienna in addition to Muri Abbey in Switzerland, where Karl and Zita's hearts are buried together. I also visited Austria's military museum, where I had the opportunity to see firsthand materials from Karl during the First World War and read some of Karl's calls for world peace. Witnessing that history gave me a greater understanding of the empire that Karl inherited and how much he sacrificed to serve and protect his people.

I began actively promoting Karl's canonization by writing online blog posts on behalf of the Blessed Karl League of Prayers for Peace Among Nations in 2018. I am inspired by the example of Karl's heroic life and like to share it with others.

16. A Witness of Courage and Public Service

Karl stands as an example of courage and humility to all of us. His openhearted and humble behavior, especially during times of hardship and distress, is worthy not only of praise but of imitation in our own lives.

Blessed Karl was a living witness of Jesus's words in Chapter 20 of Matthew's Gospel: "Whoever wishes to be great among you shall be your servant; whoever wishes to be first among you shall be your slave."

In the same Gospel chapter, Jesus also said the unforgettable words: "The last will be first, and the first will be last."

Blessed Karl was someone whose title and

heritage put him first in the world—yet he freely chose to serve and to put himself last.

His example demonstrates that we can all practice heroic virtue and be a force of love and goodness in the world no matter what our life situation. Karl was a man whose life was defined by willing responses to demands for selfless service—as a husband, father, soldier and statesman. Love gave him the courage to meet all of his tasks with a willing heart.

That is why Blessed Karl is one of the greatest national leaders to emerge in the 20th century and is truly a saint for our time.

17. Prayers to Blessed Karl

For Blessed Karl's Intercession

O Blessed Emperor Karl, you accepted the difficult tasks and burdensome challenges that God gave you during your life. In every thought, decision and action you trusted always in the Holy Trinity.

We pray to you to intercede for us with the Lord our God to give us faith and courage, so that even in the most difficult situations of our earthly lives we may not lose heart, but continue faithfully in the footsteps of Christ. Ask for us the grace that our hearts may be molded into the likeness of the Sacred Heart of Jesus.

Help us to work with compassion and strength for the poor and needy, to fight with courage for peace in our homes and in the world, and in every situation to trustingly place our lives in the hands of God, until we reach Him, as you did, through Christ our Lord. Amen

Prayer to God for the Faith of Blessed Karl

God Our Father, through the gift of Blessed Karl you have given us an example to follow. In extremely difficult times he performed his burdensome tasks without ever losing his faith. He always followed your Son, the true king.

He led a humble life, sincerely loving the poor and giving himself heart and soul to the search for peace. Even when his life was in danger he trusted in you, putting his life in your hands. Almighty and merciful God, by the intercession of Blessed Karl, we pray that you may give us his unconditional faith to support us in our most difficult situations, and the courage to always follow the example of your only Son.

Open our hearts to the poor, and strengthen our commitment for peace within our families and among all peoples. We ask this through Christ our Lord. Amen.

18. About the Author

The author stands next to a bust of Karl in the Imperial crypt in Vienna in 2017.

Zita Ballinger Fletcher (also known by the pen name Zita Steele) is a journalist and author of fiction and nonfiction books. She frequently writes on military history. She was named after Empress Zita of Austria and later chose Blessed Karl as her Confirmation namesake.

Sources

- "The Path to Leadership," Field Marshal Bernard Law Montgomery (1961).

- "Catholic Prayers to Saintly Germanic Kings & Queens," Marie Noel (2014).

- "Kaiser Karl: Persönliche Aufzeichnungen, Zeugnisse und Dokumente," Erich Feigl. Amalthea (1984).

- "A Heart for Europe: The Lives of Emperor Charles and Empress Zita of Austria-Hungary," James and Joanna Bogle (2000).

- "Eternal Love: The Hearts of Karl and Zita Enshrined Together," Zita Ballinger Fletcher, blog article: Blessed Karl League of Prayers for Peace Among Nations (March 12, 2018).

- "Karl: A Ruler of Peace," Zita Ballinger Fletcher, blog article: Blessed Karl League of Prayers for Peace Among Nations (July 3, 2018).

- "Blessed Karl and the Sacred Heart of Jesus," Zita Ballinger Fletcher, blog article: Blessed Karl League of Prayers for Peace Among Nations (July 20, 2018).

- "Blessed Karl: A Humble King," Zita Ballinger Fletcher, blog article: Blessed Karl League of Prayers for Peace Among Nations (Oct. 7, 2018).

- "Blessed Karl: A Man for All Peoples," Zita Ballinger Fletcher, blog article: Blessed Karl League of Prayers for Peace Among Nations (Dec. 6, 2018).

- "Blessed Karl: A True Soldier," Zita Ballinger Fletcher, blog article: Blessed Karl League of Prayers for Peace Among Nations (June 29, 2019).

- "Blessed Karl: Poor in Spirit," Zita Ballinger Fletcher, blog article: Blessed Karl League of Prayers for Peace Among Nations (Oct. 4, 2019).

- "Zita, the Last Empress of Austria, Dies in Swiss Exile at 96," The Associated Press in the International Herald Tribune (March 1989).

www.ingramcontent.com/pod-product-compliance
Lightning Source LLC
Chambersburg PA
CBHW031002090426
42737CB00008B/649